The FACT ATTACK series

Awesome Aliens
Beastly Bodies
Cool Cars
Crazy Creatures
Crucial Cricket
Dastardly Deeds
Deadly Deep
Devastating Dinosaurs
Dreadful Disasters
Fantastic Football
Gruesome Ghosts
Incredible Inventions
Mad Medicine
Magnificent Monarchs
Nutty Numbers
Remarkable Rescues
Rowdy Rugby
Spectacular Space
Super Spies
Vile Vampires

FACT ATTACK

DASTARDLY DEEDS

IAN LOCKE

MACMILLAN CHILDREN'S BOOKS

First published 1998 by Macmillan Children's Books

This edition published 2012 by Macmillan Children's Books
a division of Macmillan Publishers Limited
20 New Wharf Road, London N1 9RR
Basingstoke and Oxford
Associated companies throughout the world
www.panmacmillan.com

ISBN 978-1-4472-2419-8

1 3 5 7 9 8 6 4 2

A CIP catalogue record for this book is available from
the British Library.

Printed and bound by CPI Group (UK) Ltd, Croydon CR0 4YY

DID YOU KNOW THAT . . .

 Devil's Island was a famous French prison on the Isles of Salvation, off the coast of South America. It was known as the worst prison in the world and was closed in the 1960s. Very few prisoners managed to escape. One of the most well known was a Doctor Bougrat. He reached the coast of South America and was about to be sent back to prison when an earthquake hit the area. His work during the disaster saved so many lives he was able to stay a free man. In the 1970s a Frenchman called Henri Charrière wrote the story of his escape from Devil's Island in the book *Papillon*, which was made into a film starring Steve McQueen and Dustin Hoffman.

30,000 people died when an earthquake struck the city of St Pierre on the Caribbean island of Martinique in 1908. The only survivor was a prisoner in the city's jail.

 In December 1996 a supermarket sausage went on trial as an imposter.

 In 1932 Harvey Bailey, a bank robber who had stolen a record $2m two years before, was beginning a game of golf at the Old Mission golf course in Kansas City, USA, when he was arrested by the FBI. The three others who were playing with him, also bank robbers, were also arrested.

In January 1997 two Italians got away with £2 million of jewels from a Paris shop. They paid for the gems with a briefcase full of cash. But only the top notes were real – the rest were toy money!

 Up to 1820 any person in Britain who owed over £20 could be put in prison for debt.

 Two thieves who broke into a chemist in Salisbury and took two walking sticks were caught after they were seen on surveillance cameras doing Charlie Chaplin impersonations!

 Until 1998 the death penalty still existed in the UK for those who had committed high treason or piracy with violence.

A prisoner who was released on bail in London became bored. He asked if he could go back into Brixton jail. A cell was found for him but he was freed again after five days. In January 1997 he went back to court to ask if he could be allowed to go back to jail.

 At the age of 16, in 1925, Stephen Dennison was sent to a reform school in New York for shoplifting a $5 box of sweets. Two years later, he was sent to a state prison. After he broke some rules, he was given extra time. He ended up spending 34 years in jail, and was only released in 1959.

 A British policeman went on trial in 1996 for stealing money from the police social club. He used the money to play a game on a fruit machine – it was called "Cops 'n' Robbers"!

An Australian tourist wrote a letter to the *Scots* magazine, saying how much the welcome at the Grianan guest house in the north of Scotland was appreciated. The same day the owner of the guest house appeared in court, charged with the murder of another guest!

 Pets were recently allowed in Italian jails. Poisonous spiders and chickens were on the list of pets which were not allowed. In Britain some prisoners are allowed to keep budgies.

 Paddington Bear was stolen from his showcase at Paddington station, London, in 1992.

Italian burglar Mareus Crespi once asked a judge to be sent back to prison. The judge had said he had to live with his mother-in-law as a punishment!

 During a trial in July 1907 in Chicago, USA, the man on trial, a Mr Billik, who had been accused of murder, is said to have hypnotized the jury to prevent the trial going ahead.

 In 1982 a man was arrested in Newtown, Powys, for stealing an empty supermarket trolley because he wanted the wheels. He was fined.

One of the oldest prisons in the world is in Athens, Greece. Socrates, the Greek philosopher, was imprisoned there almost 2,500 years ago.

 After his escape from a POW camp in the Boer War in 1899, Winston Churchill had a £25 reward, dead or alive, placed on his head.

 Michael Mellor posed as a fake traffic policeman on a motorway in England for eight months in 1994. He would stop drivers and tell them off for their poor driving. He was eventually found out and fined £400.

 In recent years over 300 road signs have been stolen in and around Selby in North Yorkshire. The favourites are *Give Way* and *Bad Bend*.

Samuel Curtis was arrested in Philadelphia in 1924 for stealing a machine full of chewing gum. The judge sentenced him to eat all 250 pieces of chewing gum in the machine, which he had to pay for. After Mr Curtis had eaten them all, he was ordered to give the machine back to the owner. He was then freed.

 Detective Eustace, who worked for the London police in Brixton, once caught a thief by posing as a statue.

 When he stayed in the Lexington Hotel in Chicago from 1927 to 1932, the American gangster Al Capone had secret caves and staircases built. This work included a wall, behind which was a vault. Since Al Capone's fortune had never really been found, there was great excitement when the vault was going to be blasted open in 1986. The event was seen on live TV in at least ten countries. After the big bang, the vault was opened and . . . there was nothing there!

 Ellsworth de France was released in 1903 from a US prison. He had spent fifteeen years in jail for stealing a penny postage stamp!

 St Nicholas (Santa Claus) is the patron saint of thieves.

On Christmas Day 1996, Dwayne
Terry, a burglar who was hungry,
decided to play Father Christmas.
He tried to get into a supermarket in
Baltimore, USA, by going down the
chimney. He got stuck and was found
by the police wedged about a metre
down the chimney of the store! He
was freed and taken into custody. He
was lucky. In Dayton, Ohio, in the
USA, a suspected burglar was found
dead in the vent of a pizza oven!

 In 1911, three men were hanged
for the murder of Sir Edmund
Berry at Greenberry Hill, London.
Their last names were Green,
Berry and Hill.

10

A 64-year-old woman in California was a senior citizen serial killer. She was found guilty of the murder of seven elderly people. She ran a boarding house and poisoned them. She then cashed their pension payments. Two more bodies were found later.

 Two valuable paintings stolen in Oxford in 1988 turned up in a rubbish skip in an Oxford street in 1990.

 Robbers in Bucharest, Hungary, once stole the police collection of photos of criminals.

Among the stranger things to have been stolen are: a train in Florida; a bungalow, stolen brick by brick, in Bloxwich, West Midlands; and a fire engine, stolen while firemen were dealing with a fire in an old leather works in Hackney, north London!

 Ruth Ellis became the last woman to be hanged in Britain, on 13 July 1955, for the murder of David Blakeley.

 "Good" and "Evil" twins exist. In Los Angeles, Chinese twin Jeane Hau, the "evil" twin, tried to kill her "good" twin sister and take over her identity. The two were so similar to look at, that they could not be told apart. The "good" twin survived to tell the story. Not long ago, in France, a "good" twin murdered his "evil" twin brother after he had committed a murder and other crimes. He decided it was the only thing he could do.

James, Duke of Monmouth, and Lord Lovat were both beheaded for treason. Strangely, both had their heads sewn back on their bodies afterwards. The Duke of Monmouth's head was sewn back on so a picture of him could be painted. This picture is now in the National Portrait Gallery in London.

 In 1933, a man in Paris tried to rob the house of an antiques dealer. The robber had a problem – his disguise was a suit of armour! The noise woke up the owner, who watched in amazement as the burglar climbed the stairs; then he knocked him down, put a small table over the fallen knight to pin him down and called the police. When the thief was asked why he had put on a suit of armour he replied he thought it would frighten the owner. The thief had another problem – part of his armour was so dented it took another day to get him out of it!

Ned Kelly, the Australian outlaw, began a life of crime stealing horses as a teenager. After three years in prison, he began to rob banks. In April 1878, the police came to arrest Ned and his brother Dan. Ned wounded one of the policemen and fled with his brother. They went into the hills where they were joined by two other outlaws. In June the Kelly gang raided a village and held about 40 hostages in the hotel. Some time later, the police, who were on their trail with the help of aboriginal trackers, came into the village.They surrounded the hotel and started shooting. The women and children inside screamed for them to stop. During the shooting, Ned escaped. The next morning, at eight o'clock, Ned walked out to the police. He wore a huge greatcoat. Almost his whole body was covered by plates of iron and an iron helmet covered his head. As he approached the police line he opened fire with his

 14

revolvers. Nine police returned the fire and hit him, but, after staggering, Kelly recovered and walked forward, continuing to fire at the police. The shooting continued for half an hour until Sergeant Steele, moving closer to Kelly, shot him twice in the legs from about ten metres. Kelly staggered and fell. Months later Ned Kelly was hanged for his crimes. His last words were "Such is life."

 The Six Million Dollar Man, the American TV series, starred Lee Majors. It was about a bionic man with super powers. The series was filmed in California in the 1970s. In December 1976 an episode was being shot at an old amusement park funhouse. In one room stood a wax mummy. It had been there over fifty years. During the filming, it was knocked and one of the mummy's arms snapped and came off. The body of a real person was found underneath the wax! The mummy was taken to Los Angeles to be looked at. The body was of a man in his thirties. He seems to have been killed in a shoot-out in 1910 and then preserved and wrapped like a mummy to hide the crime. The body was buried in 1977. The crime remains unsolved.

 A record 258 prisoners escaped from one prison in France during World War Two, as the Resistance, helped by British planes, blew open the jail.

 The famous Spanish author of *Don Quixote*, Cervantes, was at times a criminal. In 1570 he killed a sheriff. His punishment was to have one of his hands cut off. He was later captured by pirates and became lame because of his ill treatment. He began writing his most famous book, *Don Quixote*, when in prison in Spain.

Sixty-two homing pigeons were stolen from a house in Lancashire; forty-three returned home within a few days.

 Three teenagers were arrested in a cemetery. They were dressed in white sheets and had been posing as ghosts, frightening the drunks at the cemetery into giving them money.

 The Great Train Robbers were sentenced to 307 years in jail in 1964. In 1965, one of the robbers, Ronald Biggs, escaped with three other prisoners from Wandsworth prison, London. He had plastic surgery on his face and fled to Australia where he became a carpenter, and later to Brazil. In 2001 he returned voluntarily to England and was jailed. He was released in 2009 on compassionate grounds.

It was the oddest murder trial ever. A Frenchman, Paul Hubert, was jailed for life in 1863 after being found guilty of murder. During the trial it seems no one said who had been murdered. Twenty-one years later the case was looked at again. It was found that Hubert had been jailed for murdering himself!

Allan Pinkerton became famous for his American detective agency. He did not start very well. He was the detective supposed to be guarding President Lincoln when he was assassinated by John Wilkes Booth in 1865.

The first criminals found to be wearing body armour in Britain were arrested in 1994.

In 1974, the British Labour Member of Parliament John Stonehouse disappeared off the coast of Florida. His clothes were found on the beach. The police thought he had drowned. In March 1975 he was suddenly spotted in Australia, and arrested by the police. He came back to England in July, where he was charged with fraud and jailed.

 It may be the world's biggest telephone bill. In 2006 a Malaysian man received a 218 trillion dollar bill.

During the flight 800 TWA aircraft disaster in December 1996 a man was arrested. He was charged with impersonating a military officer. Although untrained, he had spent two and a half days directing the rescue helicopters.

 Dr Crippen was an American doctor who murdered his wife in London. He cut up her body and put the bits under the floor of his house. The police nearly missed catching him. In 1910 he tried to escape to Canada with his girlfriend Ethel le Neve. He was caught when he became the first criminal to be identified by the sending of a radio message. Brought back to England, he was tried, found guilty of murder and hanged.

An American man was jailed for six months after he admitted that he had put banana skins down on the floors of the offices of forty-five companies in Chicago, then deliberately slipped on them, blaming the companies for negligence and collecting damages.

 "Goldbrick" Tony, an English criminal, needed £100,000. The answer was simple – he ordered the money from a printer! Tony's special pound notes were printed "Bank of Engford" and he even put his name on all the notes to show they were fake. The funny thing was, people took his money for things he bought. The police took Tony to court and he was sent to jail for three years.

 The crime organization the Mafia is said to be named after the saying in Italian "Death to the French is Italy's cry". The initials spell MAFIA.

In the 1940s an American boy was found in Wilmington counterfeiting nickel coins by melting down his lead soldiers.

 Ernest Coveley of London robbed fourteen banks and building societies, using cucumbers! He wrapped two cucumbers in a plastic bag and waved them about like a sawn-off shotgun. This convinced the staff he was serious, and they gave money to him. After twelve robberies he ate his first "gun" in a sandwich, then went out and bought some new cucumbers.

 In 1790 the *Pandora* ship was sent from Portsmouth, England, to track down the mutineers from the now famous mutiny on the *Bounty*. The expedition easily found the fourteen mutineers who had stayed behind at Tahiti. These men were clapped in irons and locked below deck for four months. The *Pandora* continued the search for the other mutineers, sailing west towards Australia. The ship was wrecked on the edge of the Great Barrier Reef off Australia in August 1791. A few of the prisoners and some of the crew escaped, but were unable to survive in the hostile climate.

 In Sweden in 1699, 300 children were accused of training cats to steal butter, cheese and bacon.

In one of the great unsolved crimes of the century, a man in the United States, D. B. Cooper, disappeared in 1971. He had hijacked a plane and demanded a $200,000 ransom. When this was given to him, he stuffed it into bags, which he put on his back. Then he put on a parachute and, over the border of the states of Washington and Oregon, he jumped out into a freezing rainstorm. No trace of him was found until 1980 when an 8-year-old boy found twelve bundles of the money while out in the country.

The last three "witches" were put to death in England in 1682. Forty years later a woman became the last to be burned to death as a witch in Scotland.

The first breath test machine, called the Drunkometer, was invented by Dr Harger in the USA. It was first used by the Indianapolis police in 1939.

 In 1933 a man was sentenced to death for murder in America. A little later he was told his sentence had been reduced to imprisonment for life. When told the news he said, "Now I can finish my jigsaw puzzle."

 Michael Mutford escaped from a Florida jail on a lawnmower. He was working near some woods in a prison camp when he took his chance.

 There are lots of detective stories where the butler is the criminal. In February 1978, the butler really did do it. He murdered an ex-Labour MP and his wife in Scotland.

When England were holding the World Cup football finals in 1966 the cup was put on show in London. It was stolen: the police found no clues and after two weeks still had no lead. Then, one night, David Corbett took his dog Pickles for a walk in Norwood, south London. David noticed a glint of something in the bushes, covered by a pile of newspapers. He walked on, but Pickles went to the pile of papers and sniffed and pawed. David called Pickles, but the dog stayed where he was. Mr Corbett went over and saw, at once, that the thing on the ground was the World Cup. He took it back to his flat and phoned the police. If it had not been for Pickles, the World Cup might not have been found. Pickles was given a major animal award, a rubber bone and £53 for food. Mr Corbett was later to receive rewards worth £6,000. Before the final, the West German team all met Pickles and touched him for good luck. Pickles had his moment of glory and was a real hero.

Prisoners dug a 120 metre long tunnel to escape from a prison camp in Germany in World War Two. The escape was the biggest during the war.

 In 1994, a US judge sent criminals to church instead of jail.

 For some unknown reason, police in New York recorded no serious crime from 10.30 on the Wednesday evening to just after 10.30 on the Friday evening in the first week of February in 1993.

People swimming in Avignon, France, in 1948 saw a man, with his jacket over his head, lying near some bushes on the beach. Everyone thought he was asleep. Each days his arms and legs moved. Sometimes his shoes were on, sometimes they were off. After some days, one swimmer pulled back the man's jacket. He was quite dead and had been battered to death. The murderer had moved the arms and legs every day to put off discovery of the murder.

 In 1992 a JCB digger was stolen and used later in the day to steal a cash dispenser with £40,000 in it from a building society in a shopping centre near Gillingham, Kent.

A shark led to a murder mystery in Australia in 1935. Fisherman Bert Hodson pulled in his line one morning and found he had caught two sharks – one, a rare Tiger shark, was, unbelievably, just finishing eating the other smaller shark! The Tiger shark was so rare, Bert took it to his brother's aquarium where it went on show. A few days later, as visitors watched, the shark was sick. To the horror of those watching, among the things that came out was the small shark, with a human arm in its mouth! The police were called and found the arm had belonged to a James Smith. A few months later, John Brady, one of Smith's friends, was tried for his murder. He was found not guilty. The real story of the murder remains unknown.

The famous picture by Leonardo da Vinci, the Mona Lisa, was stolen from the Louvre art gallery in Paris in August 1911. The picture was missing for two years. It was found when the thief admitted he had the painting in Italy. He was given one year and fifteen days in prison.

 When twelve Danish prisoners escaped from jail in 1995 it was shown on TV. They got out when a bulldozer knocked down the wall. A little later, one of the prisoners asked to go back to jail – he did not like it on the outside.

 In July 1976, thieves dug tunnels through the sewers in Nice, in the south of France. They got as far as one of the main banks, where they stole a record £6 million.

A prisoner in Parkhurst jail on the Isle of Wight did not manage to fool the doctors. He said he had jaundice, a disease which makes the skin go yellow. He had actually spent two days painting his body with yellow felt tip marker.

About a hundred years ago the Emperor of Ethiopia used an electric chair as a throne!

The *vendetta*, when one person kills another for revenge, may have begun on the island of Corsica. In the early 1900s seventeen people were killed in a vendetta on the island in an argument over who owned a chestnut tree!

John Lee became "the man they could not hang" in 1885. A Miss Keyse had been stabbed to death in her home, The Glen, at Babbacombe in Devon. The house was then set on fire. Lee, who was a servant in the house, was arrested by the police. He was tried, found guilty of the murder and sentenced to be hanged. After breakfast on the morning of the execution, Lee was led to the yard of Exeter prison. A black bag was placed on his head and the rope put around his neck as he stood on the trapdoor. When the hangman pulled the lever – nothing happened! The trapdoor did not move, even when the hangman stamped on it. Some changes were made and the lever was pulled. Again nothing happened! A carpenter was called in and some of the trapdoor was planed down. But, even at the third try, the door would not open. Lee had the rope and bag taken off and was led back to his cell. A little later the sentence of death was lifted. He stayed in prison until 1907. Later he went to America, where he died in 1933.

The guards on night patrol in Parkhurst prison on the Isle of Wight wore thick-soled felt shoes, so they could not be heard by the prisoners. One night about seventy-five years ago, while moving without a sound, a guard was very surprised to see a prisoner coming down an iron stair! All the prisoners were supposed to be locked up for the night. When the guard went with the prisoner to his cell, he found that the door was closed and locked. All the bars on the windows were in place. The floor had not been dug up. How the prisoner got out remained a mystery, and he wasn't going to tell!

 Captain Thomas Blood, dressed as a priest, went to the Royal Treasure Room of the Tower of London in 1675. There was only one guard. Blood overpowered him, then stole the Crown jewels. Putting them in a sack, he tried to escape. He was caught before he left the Tower of London. King Charles II was so impressed by the daring deed of Captain Blood, that he said that Blood was not to be hanged for his crime. More than that, he gave this royal burglar a pension of £300 a year!

 The American actress Zsa Zsa Gabor had a designer striped dress made in case she had to go to jail for slapping a policeman in Los Angeles. She was later sent to jail for three days.

 A Californian woman had a son who was a fireman. She noticed that he did not have a lot of work and might lose his job. So she began to light brush fires so he would be busy. Found out, she was sent to prison for 120 days.

The first criminal on the run to be caught by the Internet was Leslie Rogg. He had escaped from a jail in the USA in 1985 and was on the run for eleven years. He was found in Guatemala in South America after his picture appeared on the Internet.

 Rosemary Abadour pretended she had a lot of money. In fact she stole over £2 million from a charity in London. She spent £780,000 on parties, £280,000 on cars and over £134,000 on maids and others to help her! She was jailed for four years in 1992 after she came back from South America to give herself up.

 In 1954 a donkey caused a murder. Jules Guily of Corsica killed his next door neighbour after his donkey wandered into his garden and the two men had a fight as a result.

During World War Two British and other prisoners escaped from their jail at Sagan, Germany, by a tunnel. The tunnel was dug while the prisoners took exercise by jumping over a vaulting horse. The story of the escape was told in the book and film *The Wooden Horse*.

 1,400 people applied for a hangman's job in Britain in 1883.

 In 1873 a man named Joshua Coppersmith was arrested in New York for trying to raise money for a new invention, a telephone. An American paper said: "Well-informed people know that it is impossible to transmit the human voice over wires . . . and that (if) it was possible to do so, the thing will be of no practical value."

The most famous horse to be stolen was Shergar. The horse had won the Derby in 1981. He was stolen from a farm in County Kildare, Ireland, on 9 February 1983. No trace has ever been found of the horse. The owners refused to pay a ransom for the horse.

 King Gustav III of Sweden thought coffee was a poison. He once sentenced a man "to death" by drinking coffee every day. The man lived to be very old.

 There were strange robberies in San Francisco in the 1940s. Large numbers of manhole covers were stolen in the city.

In 1803 in Sydney, Australia, Joseph Samuels was about to be hanged. The rope broke twice. The third time he was hanged, but nothing happened – he just "hung about" in the air for a bit. He was let off.

 A nurse was sentenced to prison for thirteen years in France in 1991. She was supposed to have been caring for a rich old woman, but instead she had locked the woman in her room for five years and in the end allowed her to die. The nurse then set about stealing the old woman's collection of art, worth £175 million. She did, in fact, sell one of the old lady's pictures to France's top museum, the Louvre in Paris, for nearly £3 million in 1988.

 In 1993 Ingrid Hannoway was taken to court in Britain. She was charged with abandoning a spider. She had tried to post a pet tarantula in a plastic container.

Only 15 prisoners survived in the Changi jail in Singapore during World War Two. One of them was the writer James Clavell. He wrote the book *King Rat* about his life in the prison. Later he wrote the screenplays for films such as *The Great Escape*.

 Seventy-five prisoners tried to escape from a prison in Mexico in 1975. They dug and dug until their tunnel was finished in April 1976. They must have made a wrong turn somewhere, because they came up in the court where many of them had been sent to jail in the first place! They were all returned to jail.

Fingerprinting was first used by an Argentine policeman in 1891. The first British person to go to jail because of his fingerprints was Harry Jackson. He had stolen six billiard balls from a house in London. His fingerprints were found, and afterwards he was found guilty. He was sentenced to six years in prison.

 Frenchwoman Charlotte Corday murdered Jean Marat, a French leader, in his bath in Paris in 1793. She stabbed him to death. The murder was to help lead to the French Revolution.

 In ancient China, robbers of tombs were sliced to death.

£2,631,784 was stolen in the Great Train Robbery at Sears Crossing, Buckinghamshire, England, on 8 August 1963. Two boys later gave police the clues they needed to find the robbers' hideout.

 Frank Mullins escaped from Edinburgh prison in June 1945 through a 30 cm hole and down a 45 cm drainpipe. He had been on a diet for weeks and, before he left his cell, had put grease, meant for a skin complaint, all over his body.

 In February 1993, Barclays Bank shut one of its branches after two robberies in two weeks. The staff had had enough.

In 1904 a jewel thief called John Smith was caught by the police in England. When they saw him the police found they had made a big mistake. Another man, from Norway, called Adolph Beck, had been put in prison seven years before for stealing the jewellery. Adolph Beck and John Smith looked exactly the same!

 The first toothbrush is said to have been made by William Addis while in the Newgate prison, London, in 1780. He made the toothbrush from bone and a few bristles of a scrubbing brush. After he was let out of jail he began selling his toothbrushes. Among the other things invented in jail was the tip of the billiard cue.

A prisoner in a US jail in the 1940s was given solitary confinement for using the electric chair as a toaster.

 In the biggest escape ever, 25,000 North Korean prisoners escaped from jails in South Korea in June 1953. The President of South Korea ordered that they be left free because he did not like the way the Korean war had ended.

 In 1970 an American writer and actor was arrested for using a "stolen" credit card. A computer had listed him as dead!

In the 1800s the town of Evanston, America, made it a crime to sell ice cream with soda on Sundays. The people who made the ice cream and soda did not want to be out of work. They thought of a way round the new law. They made the ice cream, then put syrup on top. They called it an ice cream sundae.

 One day in Italy a thief stole a case from a man's car. The man had stopped to change a tyre after a puncture. When the thief left, the man found a lottery ticket the thief had dropped. He found the thief and gave him the ticket – worth £25,000 – telling him he did not want a reward for finding it.

In England in 1644 it was a crime to eat anything on Christmas Day!

 For nearly two years people working as printers of banknotes in Argentina made their own money! In 1989, it was found that up to four out of every ten banknotes were fakes.

 In the 1900s a newcomer came to a place in New South Wales, Australia. One night he had a dream. He could not get the dream out of his mind. He dreamed he had seen the murder of a farmer called Shaun Cott. In the end, he went to the police and told them about his dream. They said Cott was missing.

The man said they should dig around the farm to find Cott's body. They did. The body of Cott, with his skull bashed in, was found. A man who worked on the farm was arrested for murder. He was later tried and hanged for the murder of Cott.

 Early on Christmas Day 1950 the coronation stone, the Stone of Scone, was stolen from the coronation chair in Westminster Abbey, London. It was returned by three Scottish Nationalists to Arbroath Abbey in Scotland in April 1951.

A scientist can tell if a criminal is left- or right-handed. In America in 1924, Harry Hoffman was found not guilty of shooting dead Maude Bauer after it was proved, at his third trial, that he was left-handed and that the real killer was right-handed.

 Butch Cassidy and the Sundance Kid, who stole over $200,000 from banks and trains across America, were supposed to have been shot dead by soldiers in Bolivia, South America, in 1909. In 1978 Butch's sister said he had not been killed, but had lived until 1937. She said two other bodies were buried in the place of Butch and the Sundance Kid.

A thief in Austria was found guilty because of his teeth. He stole gold being used by a dentist for fillings. Before he left the dentist's he bit on an apple there. Finding it sour, he ate only part of it and left it behind. The dentist saw the apple, and made a cast of the marks made by the teeth. Only a little later the thief was caught when he went to the dentist.

 In 1987 the body of the man who is said to have shot President Kennedy was dug up. A British writer said that it was not Lee Harvey Oswald in the grave, but a Russian spy.

The daughter of one of the leaders of Romania in the 1930s was poisoned by cyanide which had been put in her tooth powder.

Some years ago, on a freezing winter's day, three teenage boys stole a woman's purse in New York. They tried to make their getaway in a way which would fool the police – they jumped on to a sheet of ice about two metres long floating on the Hudson river, which runs through New York. They remained stranded on the ice until they were rescued by a police helicopter!

It was only by one vote that a group of Frenchmen decided that King Louis XVI should have his head cut off by the guillotine in 1793.

Over three hundred years ago, John, Richard and Joan Perry were hanged on a hill in England for the murder of William Harrison, who had been missing from the time he went out with the three of them. All three said they were innocent. Two years later William Harrison turned up. He said he had been kidnapped and sold as a slave to a Turkish doctor.

 Thieves in Torrance, California, once stole a glass factory! They emptied the building, then took it to bits and drove away with it.

 William Gillen, aged 26, was arrested by police in Glasgow for trying to rob a bank. The police put him into an identity parade. As no one from the bank could recognize him, he might have gone free, but he then called out from the line-up, "Hey, don't you recognize me?"

William Saunders took fourteen people hostage in the high-rise office of a big business in New York. Saunders held them all in one room. After a time one of the hostages asked to leave the room for a drink of water. Saunders said OK. One by one, the remaining thirteen of Saunders' hostages asked to leave the room for a glass of water. They never returned.

 A burglar who broke into a flat in California left a five-page note signed Prince Eddie. He cleaned and tidied the flat. All he took was a pair of curtains, but he put a new set of curtains in their place!

In 1985 Alberto Mesa was arrested by the Miami police. He was not only walking by people's houses with no clothes on, he was carrying a woman's severed head! As the police came close to him, Mesa screamed, "I killed her. She's the Devil."

 In the year 1962, 313,000 people were arrested for being drunk in the Polish capital Warsaw.

 The first Sherlock Holmes story by Sir Arthur Conan Doyle was *The Study in Scarlet*. Conan Doyle's first name for Holmes was Sherringford and the first name for Dr Watson, Ormond Sacher. He changed his mind and gave them new names.

Because of a mistake in the law in Britain, any patient who can escape from a mental hospital and remain uncaught for four weeks can go free.

 Harold Longhams, who had spent time in prison, was found not guilty at his second trial of the murder, by strangling, of Rose Robinson. She had been found murdered on the night of 28 November 1943. Longhams had only four half-fingers on his hand and it was believed it was not possible for him to strangle her. In 1963 Longhams, who was dying of cancer, walked into the offices of *The People* newspaper and confessed to the murder.

 It is against the law to use plastic bags in parts of Afghanistan.

A headmaster and teacher in India were arrested by the police in 1966. They had kept twenty-one students in chains for three days because they were not studying!

 An American thief thought he could escape from the policemen who were chasing him by hiding in bushes. He soon came out, though. The bushes were crawling with ants and he got covered in them. He rushed out scratching all over and gave himself up!